POWER DECK

75 ANIMALS TO AWAKEN YOUR PERSONAL MAGIC

ALYSON CHARLES

Illustrations by
WILLIAN SANTIAGO

INTRODUCTION

Hi, Soul Family!

Welcome to *Animal Power Deck: 75 Animals to Awaken Your Personal Magic*. In this deck, you will connect with 75 power animals and discover their energetic medicines, sacred wisdom, and empowering messages. Allow the deck to guide you toward the miracles, transformation, richness, and unconditional love that your soul is so ready for, while honoring these animals at the same time.

WORKING WITH ANIMAL POWER

Every animal possesses energetic healing properties, signature traits, and life-changing teachings. Animals give us strength, guide us through life, remind us of our own internal power, and are our teachers. For many thousands of years, sacred wisdom traditions have deeply honored the medicine and care that animals provide to us.

No matter their appearance or reputation, each animal is sacred, whether it's a leech or an elephant. When we work with the spirit of an animal—the energetic aspect of the animal—with reverence and respect, we greatly enhance our lives. There are many ways we can access the guidance of power animals: through meditation, conversation, observation, shamanic journeying, sacred rituals, and other practices. In this deck, I'll guide you through invocations that will allow you to tap into each animal's energy with integrity and honor.

These animals are our helpers and guides. These generous, loving beings can assist us and support our rise. Each and every animal possesses beauty, intelligence, and divine power. We are all one, every living being, whether tiny or slimy, a massive ocean mammal, a desert-roaming creature, or a wild soaring bird. Every animal has an energetic essence within it that contains certain wisdoms, energetic medicines, and teachings for us. They are our brothers and sisters, as we are theirs.

Working with animals and their powers has always been a planetary practice, celebrated in many ways by many cultures.

It's vital to honor that, for many thousands of years, sacred wisdom traditions have deeply revered the medicine and care that animals provide to us. Mystics, sages, shamans, druids, and other spiritual aspirants throughout the world have recognized how being consciously aware of what animals are presenting, and what healing properties and wisdom they are bringing forth, can greatly inform our decisions and deeply empower and enhance our direction in life.

This card deck is rooted in my very close relationship with the power animal world. After my divine intervention and spiritual awakening, the first guides in the unseen realms who entered to support me in my new way of experiencing life were power animals. My close and sacred connection with them continued to be dominant through my work as a Shaman, having worked with them and been a voice for them in countless ways, including leading many thousands through guided shamanic journeys where they are able to meet and communicate with their power animal helpers, often for the first time.

My shamanic path primarily consists of my direct connection with Great Mother Earth, the divine wisdom, and the love and truth that lives within me and Great Spirit/Source. I live in devotion to the callings I am given, and it is through my deep relationship with the animals and my devotion to the calls that this deck is now with you!

HOW TO USE THIS DECK

As you work with this card deck, you will be immersing in blessed energetic transmissions; ancient animal wisdom; and eye-opening, soul-expanding messages and guidance. This deck carries sacred teachings, and it is important to treat it with care and respect. When you engage with your deck, say hello to it and all the animals. Introduce yourself and express a kind message from your heart. If you feel called, you can light a piece of sustainable palo santo or cedar and waft the smoke stream around the deck. This signifies you are ready and willing to work with this deck with honor. You can also sing to the deck, use a drum or rattle, or do whatever you feel called to do to align your energy with the deck's energy.

Each of the 75 cards includes the animal's name, an evocative illustration, and a power proverb to illuminate the animal's energy and medicine. Turn to the pages in this booklet for a description of the creature's medicinal properties and an invocation—an energetic practice to open up lines of communication and divine support between you and the animal—to connect with its sacred medicine. You can speak the invocation out loud, say it in your head as a silent prayer, or write it in your journal. I've also included a short glossary at the back of this booklet, with definitions for terms I use throughout the deck.

There are a variety of ways you can commune with this deck. You can pull a card or cards each day to see what the animals reveal, or you can look through the deck to find the animal that's calling to you in the moment. You can keep the deck on your nightstand and pull a card before you go to bed to see which animal wants to work with you during dreamtime. If a certain animal is coming up for you—appearing in your dreams or in real life—find that card in the deck to learn more about what it means.

I recommend starting your day by taking a moment to sit in sacred space, holding the deck in your hands with your eyes closed and connecting with your heart center and breath. Let your intuition guide your practice. You may want the animals with the messages and medicines you need to randomly reveal themselves to you, or you may want to ask the deck a specific question before pulling a card. Here are some questions you might consider asking before you pull a card:

"What medicine does my heart most need today?"

"What is this situation trying to teach me?"

"What animal will best guide me as I _____ (pitch my idea to my team, communicate with my mother-in-law, have a difficult conversation with a loved one, etc.)?"

"What teaching would most empower my soul?"

Once you are ready, knock on the deck three times, then shuffle the deck until the card or cards begin to call to you. You will know when a card is revealing because you will feel noticeably drawn to that card in the deck; it might even exit the deck with such force that it lands on the floor. What is key is always tuning in to your intuition and sensing which card is the one attempting to communicate with you. Pull as many cards as you want!

There are no set-in-stone rules here; it's all about you learning to trust what you need each day. Perhaps one day you'll simply want to pull one card and carry that card with you to remind you of the animal's message, and another day you'll want to pull four cards and place them at your altar space to return to at various times during the day. If one animal lives at your altar for an extended period of time, you can place other objects near it that you feel the animal would like, such as a flower, stone, crystal, feather, or herbs.

To dive deeper into the unique energy medicine and the reason an animal showed up for you, go to the entry in this guidebook of the animal or the animal cards you pulled. There you will find additional notes on their teachings and powers, along with a sacred invocation you can say aloud to specifically call that animal forth to work with you. Reciprocity is important, so thank the animals for their love and empowering support on a regular basis. In opening up your communication lines with them, perhaps an additional way you can share your love and support of them on the Earth plane or astral plane will reveal. If it does, please honor the idea that presented and go for it.

No matter whether you're just beginning your inward quest or you're a seasoned spiritual practitioner, this card deck is a tool to help you unlock your true and infinite potential by connecting to the sacred power of the animal world. The highest level of care, energy, and blessings went into cocreating this deck with the power animals, and it is my intention that working with it expands your ability to feel self-empowered, fulfilled, whole, and connected to the ever-present miracles of your Earth walk and the Universes around you.

Let's begin.

—Alyson Charles

ALLIGATOR

TAKE INTUITIVE ACTION

Alligator represents divine timing. Alligators conserve energy as they wait for the precise moment when they intuitively know to take action with every ounce of their might. When the moment calls for it, they can go from total stillness to lightning-quick speed. If you are wondering whether you should make your move, alligator is your sign to go for it! Maybe you've been thinking about activating a new project or stepping into a new practice or relationship. Or perhaps you've been thinking about the opposite—about stopping or releasing something from your life. The time to go for the goal is right now.

INVOCATION TO ACTIVATE ALLIGATOR MEDICINE:

"Sacred alligator friend, thank you for revealing that the time to act is *now*. I invite you to continue working with and empowering me so that my next steps are taken from a place of love, confidence, and clarity. I am ready to move forward with power and grace."

ANT

KEEP GOING

Ant teaches you persistence. Ant is committed to doing whatever it takes to carry a project or plan to completion. When ant appears in your life, it reminds you to steadfastly adhere to a strategy as you pursue your long-term goals. Work with ant to improve your stamina, when you feel frustrated by a lack of instant gratification, or when you've hit a place in your path where you feel tired, confused, or overwhelmed. You might have to prove yourself by going through rites of passage in order to attain your goal. Ant medicine reminds you to keep going. Believe in yourself and press forward!

INVOCATION TO ACTIVATE ANT MEDICINE:

"Blessed ant, anytime I feel tired or weak, I invite you to work with me in awakening my grand ability to remain focused, strong, and persistent. I allow in any healing or blessings you may have for me at this time. And so it is."

ARMADILLO

TRUST YOURSELF

Steadily moving toward achieving true independence and sovereignty may be the greatest path you will walk. Armadillo teaches you how to have healthy boundaries along the way so that you can walk this path with integrity and clarity. Armadillo medicine helps you trust yourself, especially when it comes to remaining in your power and revealing your unique personality and gifts while in relationships. Are you allowing someone to exert more influence over you than you should? Or are you leaning so far into independence that you lack human connection and receiving? Take an honest look at where you are on the sovereign path and know that armadillo is here to walk with you toward even richer personal trust and power.

INVOCATION TO ACTIVATE ARMADILLO MEDICINE:

"Loving armadillo, thank you for reminding me of my sovereignty. If there are any codependent cords between me and someone else, help clear them now with honor and ease. I trust I am finding my way to embodying my greatest personal power and invite you to bless this illuminated pathway forward."

BAT

FACE YOUR FEARS

Is there a fear you've been suffering from that you are finally ready to transcend? Is there something dark that you are giving too much of your power away to? Bat is a most potent ally for entering caves that hold something you've been avoiding because it feels scary. Bat medicine may feel intimidating, but you can fully trust that it carries deep love. It allows you to transcend worlds within yourself so that you can greatly uplevel in your life. Through the alchemy of transmuting fear to love, you will discover true self-worth and honor, the foundational basis for healthy dynamics in all facets of life. With bat flying by your side, you will go deeper than ever before to address the fears holding you back and will emerge with love and power.

INVOCATION TO ACTIVATE BAT MEDICINE:

"Sacred bat, thank you for revealing your love and respect for me. As I traverse the caves holding my darkest fears, teach me to alchemize with grace. Guide me in facing my fears so they no longer hold power over me. I am prepared for my sacred rebirth and ready to embody my wholeness."

BEAR

SURRENDER TO TRUTH

Bear teaches you that now is the time to courageously open up and step into your truth. Bear medicine is a most grounded, powerful, and comforting ally to have when your life appears to be turning upside down. When you grow exhausted of the cycles of suffering and allow your true calling to emerge, it can feel cataclysmic and challenging. Allow bear to be your ally as you move through this process. Envision yourself sitting in front of a bear with your back facing its belly. Allow your whole being to fully release into the bear's loving support as you lean into it and place your back against its belly and chest. Let it all go. Connect with your breath and heart. Tune in to the love that bear has for you and, with bear's support, become aware of ways that you can be more fully yourself in order to allow true fulfillment to emerge.

INVOCATION TO ACTIVATE BEAR MEDICINE:

"Trusted bear, thank you for allowing me to experience your support and open myself up to surrendering to my calling, and the never-ending guidance of Source. I have all the courage I need to be my most authentic, fulfilled, and powerful self."

BEAVER

BUILD WITH INTEGRITY

Beaver represents healthy relationships, teamwork, and building a solid foundation so that you can go after dreams. Beaver teaches that now may be an ideal time to breathe life into a new project or into an old one you've given up on but know you should activate again. Beaver reminds you to be aware of the intention and energy foundation that informs how you teach, share, and build projects. Consider what the driving force is behind what you bring to the world. Ask yourself, "Is my ego fueling these steps?" Working with beaver's medicine, tune in to whether you are acting from a place of wholeness and integrity, or dysfunction and insecurity. This exercise will ensure that your work is grounded in honor, which is especially important if you are in a position of power or leadership.

INVOCATION TO ACTIVATE BEAVER MEDICINE:

"Sacred beaver, work with me to ensure I am building, creating, and leading with wholeness, truth, and integrity. If I slip into unconscious or harmful ways, lovingly bring me into conscious awareness and give me the ability to make a positive change. I receive these blessings from you now and moving forward."

BEE

CELEBRATE LIFE

When life seems monotonous, the bee flies in to remind you there is always something to celebrate. Holding this card to your heart, think of three things that bring richness to your life. Take a moment to honor and celebrate them. When you make time for celebration and gratitude, you open yourself up to new inspiration and blessings. Bee reminds you that the possibilities are truly infinite.

INVOCATION TO ACTIVATE BEE MEDICINE:

"Blessed bee, thank you for reminding me to celebrate the blessings in my life. I call on you to deliver any new ideas or inspirations that I should be the conduit for, and I invite your medicine blessings of pollination, fertility, and celebration to infuse them."

BEETLE

THINK OPTIMISTICALLY

When the beetle shows up, it's a good time to pause and reflect on the direction and quality of your thoughts. The beetle, especially the scarab beetle, reminds you to keep your thoughts pointed toward the sun. In other words, if you have a tendency to slip into worry, victim mentality, or a defeatist attitude, it's time to consider how you can retrain your mind to think more optimistically. When you notice yourself entering into a cycle of difficult emotions, take a breath and see whether you can bring more optimism, more sun, to your thinking. This will take practice, but if followed with devotion, a new way of life awaits.

INVOCATION TO ACTIVATE BEETLE MEDICINE:

"Sacred beetle, thank you for reminding me of the power of my thoughts. I invite you to work with me in keeping my thoughts and visions pointed toward the sun, especially when it comes to _____. I allow myself to fully receive your guidance and energetic medicine."

BLACK JAGUAR

CLAIM YOUR SPIRITUAL POWER

The mystical black jaguar enters your life when it is time for you to stop suppressing your power or giving it away to others. Black jaguar calls you to reclaim your power by leaning more fully into your spiritual gifts and abilities. It's time to take an honest look at the ways you've been distracting yourself from your Earth mission (purpose) to ensure your energy and actions are aligning with your deepest calling. Black jaguar brings a very strong and focused energy and love, and calls on you to tune in to nature, especially the moon, to activate your spiritual medicine. Now is the time.

INVOCATION TO ACTIVATE BLACK JAGUAR MEDICINE:

"Powerful black jaguar, if I am doing things that prevent me from recognizing my true spiritual power, I ask that you reveal them to me with grace and ease. Walk with me in seeing truth so I may reclaim my power and live my most miraculous life. And so it is."

BUFFALO

SHARE ABUNDANCE

Sacred buffalo shares lessons about abundance, generosity, and gratitude. Buffalo medicine helps you tune in to the abundance in your own life so that you can share it with those around you. Close your eyes, take a few breaths until you feel centered, and then ask yourself, "Whose life can I empower right now, and how should that support be provided to them?" When you allow yourself to be present to all the abundance in your own life and trust that you have been abundantly provided for, you can share generously with others from a place of energy and joy. It feels great to support other beings in their Earth experience, and this is your reminder to do so now.

INVOCATION TO ACTIVATE BUFFALO MEDICINE:

"Blessed buffalo, thank you for reminding me of the abundance in my life. Thank you for walking with me so that I can embody an abundant energy that will allow me to share more generously with others. And so it is."

BULL

STEP FORWARD

Now is a powerful time for you to step forward toward a grand goal, especially when you're in a position of leadership. Bull medicine offers a balance of divine masculine energy (passion, strength, stamina, and confidence) and divine feminine energy (kindness, trust, and the ability to delegate). Bull also reminds you to remain open-minded as you pursue your dreams. Having a clear vision is great, but if you become overly stubborn or inflexible, you may miss an opportunity for your plan to expand into something far greater than you ever imagined!

INVOCATION TO ACTIVATE BULL MEDICINE:

"Powerful bull, be with me as I step into greater leadership. I am ready for my passion and stamina, along with my ability to trust and be kind, to be activated. When I need the strength to keep going as I pursue my goals, empower me. Thank you."

BUTTERFLY

LIGHTEN UP

Butterfly reminds you to take a lighter approach to things, especially during periods of transformation or transition. When you're going through big or sudden changes and things feel heavy and serious, tune in to butterfly medicine to lift your emotional experience. How can you introduce more ease, lightheartedness, and joy into your life at this moment? Transformation may bring discomfort, but remember that it is temporary. Trust that the discomfort is simply due to stretching and ascending into a more evolved you! Keep butterfly by your side to remind you that you can navigate the transition with lightness and grace.

INVOCATION TO ACTIVATE BUTTERFLY MEDICINE:

"Sacred butterfly, when I fall into an emotional state that is heavy or serious for too long, may I think of you in joyous flight. I receive your uplifting medicine as I evolve with grace and ease!"

CAMEL

ACTIVATE INNER COSMOS

When camel reveals, it is a time to explore the layers of consciousness within yourself. You live in an infinite Universe, and your ability to evolve is also infinite. Camel appears to help you discover the next steps for your exploration of your inner cosmos. Camel teaches you to view your Earth experience as an ongoing adventure, embrace experiences with curiosity and positivity, and remember that you are here to learn and grow! Life is not about getting things perfectly; it's about being willing to keep moving forward calmly and confidently.

INVOCATION TO ACTIVATE CAMEL MEDICINE:

"Dearest camel, I am ready to receive your medicines of curiosity and commitment as my inner power and infinite consciousness expand. Thank you for letting me know that now is an ideal time to embrace positivity and confidence. I know I have all I need to succeed."

CLAM

DISCOVER HAPPINESS

You've heard the saying "happy as a clam," and one of clam's main medicines is happiness. Clam appears to help you reclaim your personal joy by taking responsibility for your emotional well-being. If you feel down, disrespected, or taken advantage of, consider what active steps you can commit to taking today that will bring about greater harmony in your life so that you can share your unique treasures. Work with clam when it's time to go deeper than what sometimes feels comfortable in order to discover what's holding you back. Sometimes anguish is a result of suppressing talents and abilities, hiding them from others and also from yourself. How can you share your happiness with the world?

INVOCATION TO ACTIVATE CLAM MEDICINE:

"Blessed clam, I am ready to understand how I am holding myself back or not taking responsibility for my true joy. I know that by facing the truth and doing the work, true inner happiness is possible. I am ready for you to guide me in the next step toward unlocking my happiness so that I may share my inner treasures with the world."

CONDOR

RECEIVE MESSAGES FROM SPIRIT

Condor represents the wisdom and power of the heart, and condor medicine will help you open your heart to spiritual messages. When condor reveals, it is an important time to be aware of any messages trying to make their way to you from Great Spirit/Source, your ancestors, or benevolent guides. Connect to condor by closing your eyes and imagining the great bird in flight. Inhale deeply, sending your breath to your heart center, the space in the center of your chest. With each exhalation, clear away any foggy or darker energies. Ask Great Spirit/Source, "What message do you have for me today?" You can also ask the same question of a particular guide or ancestor. Condor medicine invites you to trust that if you leap into the unknown, you will soar with the support of Great Spirit/Source beneath your wings at all times.

INVOCATION TO ACTIVATE CONDOR MEDICINE:

"Sacred condor, show me how to open my heart to the messages of Great Spirit/Source. I am ready to be in tune with the unseen so I can cocreate in the most divine ways with the Universe. I now fully receive any medicine or guidance you have for my path moving forward."

COYOTE

ILLUMINATE YOUR ILLUSIONS

Coyote urges you to trust yourself. When coyote appears, it's time to consider whether you've been ignoring signs or communications from your soul alerting you to falsehoods in your life. Is there something you have been scared to acknowledge or face? Call on coyote to help dissolve illusions so that you may awaken to the truths that are trying to present. When you strip away illusions, you can embrace a brighter future with clarity. When you commit to seeing truth, the delusions and false narratives that once held power over you no longer will, and you will be able to face whatever comes up with beauty and grace. For additional empowerment, call upon coyote for its guidance at night before you go to sleep.

INVOCATION TO ACTIVATE COYOTE MEDICINE:

"Dear coyote friend, as I learn to break through illusion, I am ready for your empowering guidance. Be with me as I am present in silence. Reveal to me aspects of my life that need to be illuminated so that I may release delusions that are not rooted in reality. And so it is."

CROW

TRUST IN TRANSFORMATION

The crow is a potent shamanic totem that represents the birthplace of creation—the void. The void is an infinite space of an empty abyss, and crow's medicine comes from this sacred space. Crow shows up to remind you to trust the process of transformation. Unexpected change can bring myriad human emotions, and crow helps you see the beauty, sacredness, and adventure in life's twists and turns. If you let yourself be held in this energy, you will soon learn to love periods of deep change and the potential for upleveling. Focus on ascension and positive transformation rather than resistance. It is up to you whether uncertainty will drag you down or catapult you up.

INVOCATION TO ACTIVATE CROW MEDICINE:

"Sacred crow, thank you for blessing me with this medicine of great change. I invite you to be with me as I let go fully into the void. I surrender all that is to Source and allow the pathway of my greatest good to reveal."

DEER

OPEN YOUR HEART POWER

Deer is a powerful totem for everything related to the heart and unconditional love. Deer medicine offers a dose of love, compassion, and healing. When you work with this animal, it can be a many-year voyage. To open yourself up to experience true love from others, you must first experience unconditional love for yourself. Everything that happens in your external life is a reflection of the wholeness, love, respect, and honor you hold for yourself. Call upon deer to activate heart medicine for you. With deer by your side, take a moment to pause, close your eyes, and send every part of yourself unconditional love.

INVOCATION TO ACTIVATE DEER MEDICINE:

"Powerful deer, thank you for being my ally. Teach me the path of the open and whole heart. I invite in any heart-healing messages or medicines that you have for me. I am ready to be fully connected to the intelligence and intuition of my heart."

DOLPHIN

OPEN UP TO EMOTIONAL HEALING

Dolphin medicine helps you navigate your emotions with clarity and curiosity, and address any repressed feelings that may be lurking just below the surface. If you've been carrying pain or tension in your body, there may be unacknowledged emotions that are trying to be heard and felt. As you call upon the healing energies of dolphin to work with you, scan your body and notice whether there are areas that feel tense. Close your eyes and ask those areas, "What do you want me to know?" Listen with curiosity and compassion. Engage in conversation with the emotions that reveal themselves. When your emotional body feels safe, healthy, and integrated, you can return to your true nature of play, joy, and love.

INVOCATION TO ACTIVATE DOLPHIN MEDICINE:

"Dear dolphin, be with me as I learn to swim in the full spectrum of my emotions with appreciation and trust. Be with me as I feel what needs to be felt, and teach me how to open more fully to play and joy. And so it is."

DRAGONFLY

TAKE NEW DIRECTIONS

Dragonfly represents adaptability, and it shows up to give you shape-shifting powers so that you can quickly change directions with ease. If there is a change you know deep down that you need to make to move toward your soul's calling, dragonfly will help you expand in a new direction. Remember, you hold infinite wisdom and multidimensional talents within you. To expand into your power, you may feel a temporary stretch from being outside your comfort zone, and dragonfly will help you release rigidity so that you can be more flexible, open, and adaptable.

INVOCATION TO ACTIVATE DRAGONFLY MEDICINE:

"Dear dragonfly, I call on you to reveal whether a new direction is best. I will heed your guidance, and I ask that you empower me with graceful adaptability so that I may step into my truth with ease."

DUCK

STEP INTO SACRED UNION

Duck is your greatest ally when you're calling forth or strengthening a partnership. Korean, Chinese, Japanese, and other Asian cultures all revere the duck for its marital fidelity, harmony, and devotion, and the duck embodies strong, sacred relationships. Take a moment now to write down all the characteristics you most want to manifest in your relationship, whether you're already in a partnership or looking for a partner. Then, place that list at your altar with the duck card from this deck. Light a candle near the duck and envision that list coming to life within your relationship. Calling on the power of duck, consider what you can do to work toward achieving these qualities.

INVOCATION TO ACTIVATE DUCK MEDICINE:

"Duck, I ask that you reveal to me anything I need to face about myself in order to experience a healthy and sacred romantic partnership. I invite your medicine to empower my union with harmony, honor, and humor."

EAGLE

TRUST YOUR HIGHEST VISION

Eagle medicine helps you soar toward a higher, more illuminated perspective so that you can see things as they are. Eagle also calls on you to take an honest look at yourself and ask, "What feels outdated or no longer aligned with the person I'm becoming?" Once you have the answer, you can release the parts of yourself that are limiting true growth. Place this card in front of you and consider a situation that feels difficult at the moment. Can you zoom out a bit to consider things from all angles? What can you learn about yourself by looking at things from a broader perspective? From this vantage point, take a moment to tune in to where you could be more loving, supportive, or understanding. Let this highest vision give you the courage to step into new ways, trusting that eagle is by your side.

INVOCATION TO ACTIVATE EAGLE MEDICINE:

"Sacred eagle, thank you for helping me see things from a new perspective. Work with me as I surrender to Great Spirit/Source and begin to live from a healthier and higher place, simply letting love be my guide."

ELEPHANT

MOVE BEYOND OBSTACLES

Elephant asks you to look at the self-imposed blocks you've consciously or unconsciously created in your life. Elephant urges you to investigate the stories, limiting beliefs, and fears that are standing in the way of your full glory. The unconscious can be very cunning, especially when you are attached to a cycle of suffering and haven't fully learned to trust that your life can be amazing. This work takes courage as you dive deeper and deeper into the patterns and beliefs that are holding you back, but this essential work could be the key to your liberation. To work with elephant medicine, begin to explore the stories you tell about yourself that keep you from thriving—why you "won't" do something, why you "can't" be the person you want to be. Allow elephant to help you begin to move beyond those obstacles so that you can live a new story.

INVOCATION TO ACTIVATE ELEPHANT MEDICINE:

"Sacred elephant teacher, I invoke your great power to assist me in removing the obstacles I've placed in my life. Give me the clarity to see where I unconsciously block my grandest power and light from shining. Reveal to me any family or friends who can be of support. Thank you."

FLAMINGO

FIND HEALTHY BALANCE

Flamingo represents healthy balance, emotional intelligence, and maintaining good relationships with family and friends. Consider whether you've been isolating yourself or taking too much on. Flamingo reminds you to reach out to loved ones for connection and support. Is there a family member or friend your soul has been urging you to reach out to? Unless you take intentional pauses to truly check in with your emotions, you may find yourself entrenched in a way of life that isn't healthy. This is your cue to get back to what's really important and nurture the relationships that bring you joy so that you can restore balance to your life.

INVOCATION TO ACTIVATE FLAMINGO MEDICINE:

"Dear flamingo friend, I invite you to walk with me as I work on having healthier relationships. If my life gets out of balance, send clear signs to remind me to reinvest in people I care about. With you by my side, I now tune in to my heart to see who I can send love to."

FOX

WELCOME NIGHTTIME MAGIC

Fox represents attunement, wisdom, and dreams, and fox medicine enhances your ability to receive divine messages and creative inspiration during the night. When fox appears, it's a good time to pay attention to the magic that reveals to you during the night or during your dreams. For the next week, make time in the evenings to sit in meditation, journal, or immerse in a spiritual practice that resonates with you in order to see what magic wants to come alive for you. When fox shows up, you can be sure that some new insight, solution, or clever idea is on its way to you!

INVOCATION TO ACTIVATE FOX MEDICINE:

"Sacred fox, I call on you to open up the gateways of nighttime magic for me while I open myself to the possibilities. Thank you for revealing that something new wants to be born in my life. I am open to receiving your messages."

FROG

TAKE THE LEAP

Frog enters when it is imperative that you tend to your emotions or leap forward. Frog medicine can help you clear away pain and anguish caused by a toxic person or situation. To work with frog energy, take healing, restorative baths and place this card where you can see it from the tub. As you soak, consider what healthy actions you can put in place to remove toxicity. Call upon frog to be with you to release hurt or pain, especially around relationships. If you're considering making a big change in your life, let frog give you an extra boost of energy so that you can officially move forward, leaving toxicity behind you. Frog will be your greatest ally as you take the leap.

INVOCATION TO ACTIVATE FROG MEDICINE:

"Dear frog, I can sense your great care for me. I wholeheartedly receive the blessings, and I allow you to cleanse toxicity in my life and empower me to move forward as a more whole and healed person."

GIRAFFE

CONNECT TO HIGHER WISDOM

Think of the giraffe's long neck, extending upward toward the sky, along with its long legs and hooves firmly connected to the ground. Giraffe reminds you to remain steadfast in the spiritual practices that keep you both grounded and connected to the higher wisdom of Source. Having a clear connection to Source allows you to keep expanding courageously into the unknown as you pursue your truth. Experiencing life in this way, connected to Earth and Source, opens you up to hearing the wisdom within you and the wisdom available to you from benevolent guides. Giraffe medicine reminds you never to settle. As long as your connection line is strong and you feel centered and clear, put your neck out there, walk tall, and go for your absolute grandest dreams.

INVOCATION TO ACTIVATE GIRAFFE MEDICINE:

"Sacred giraffe, thank you for encouraging me to live more boldly. I allow my connection lines to Source, Earth, and the wisdom within me to grow stronger. Work with me as I find joy, expansion, and ease in the unknown."

HAWK

REMEMBER YOUR MISSION

Hawk flies in to remind you of your Earth mission and to keep you focused on the bigger picture. Are you allowing yourself to get pulled toward experiences and people that keep you from pursuing your soul calling? Take a moment to honestly ask yourself whether you've been distracting yourself to avoid doing the soul work you need to do. You might unconsciously focus on outside issues to put off doing the real work that needs to be done on yourself. Hawk tells you that it's time to refocus on what's truly important. You cannot outrun your Earth mission forever, and with hawk by your side, you now have an incredibly powerful ally to support you as you prepare to fly higher than ever before.

INVOCATION TO ACTIVATE HAWK MEDICINE:

"Sacred hawk, whenever I get pulled too far into distraction, I ask that you assist me in getting back on track with the soul work I need to do so that I may pursue my Earth mission. I open myself up to enhanced psychic abilities and remember my soul's original intention. And so it is."

HORSE

EMBRACE NEW ADVENTURE

When horse arrives in your life, you can be sure that something new and exciting is on the horizon. Horse medicine activates enhanced personal power and adventure. Do those essences resonate deeply with your soul? If so, open yourself up to having a new adventure in life. Holding this card to your heart, ask yourself three questions: "Where have I been wanting to go?" "What new life experience would I like to have?" and "What true divine power inside of me am I ready to share?" Horse encourages you to expand into greater freedom with the adventures of life and to experience greater personal power through self-discovery.

INVOCATION TO ACTIVATE HORSE MEDICINE:

"Dear horse, I invite you to work with me on my pathway moving forward as I embrace adventure and discover my personal power. I now open myself up to new experiences and welcome all they will teach me."

HUMMINGBIRD

RECEIVE THE SWEETNESS OF LIFE

Hummingbird may be a small creature, but do not underestimate the power of its potent medicine. Hummingbird arrives to help you experience awe, love, and joy, and to remind you of the sweetness of life. When hummingbird appears, it's vital that you take time to look around and see that miracles are everywhere. Place this card in your pocket or bag, take a walk to open your eyes to the beauty of the world, and give gratitude for the endless miracles of life. Practicing gratitude is a powerful way to lift yourself out of a bad mood or break out of a rut. Bask in the beauty and sweetness that surround you.

INVOCATION TO ACTIVATE HUMMINGBIRD MEDICINE:

"Sacred hummingbird friend, thank you for reminding me that I can always access immense joy. Teach me how to see the sweetness in everything and to keep my heart open."

JELLYFISH

FLOW WITH EASE

Jellyfish teaches you to remain calm and go with the flow. Have you been resisting your true path or fighting against the inevitable? If you have set an intention and asked for clear guidance from your heart and Source, it is safe to trust the process as it unfolds. This is when your faith is put to the test. If things don't go exactly as you expect and you begin to resist the path, you are exerting unnecessary time and energy. Stay connected to your heart and follow your soul calling, letting things unfold as they will. Let go of trying to control things, and flow through your journey with ease.

INVOCATION TO ACTIVATE JELLYFISH MEDICINE:

"Sacred jellyfish, teach me how to flow and trust in the process. Even when the path looks different than I think it should, work with me so that I can enjoy the experience and flow with ease. And so it is."

KANGAROO

ELIMINATE DISTRACTION

Kangaroo is known for its physical prowess and ability to connect with the grounding energy of Earth to remain focused. Kangaroo appears to help you become more aware of the distractions you are allowing to take you out of your power. It's time to get real with yourself and put an end to the distractions. Close your eyes and envision the diversions that keep you from making progress, then imagine yourself jumping past them as you take a powerful leap toward attaining your goal. Sometimes we add distractions or procrastinate to protect ourselves from potential failure or criticism, but you need to ask yourself what is more important: playing it safe or courageously going for the life of your dreams?

INVOCATION TO ACTIVATE KANGAROO MEDICINE:

"Dear powerful kangaroo ally, thank you for this call to action. I commit to seeing what distractions are at play in my life. I will stay present and grounded in my body so that I may attain my next goal with greater efficiency, joy, and ease."

KOALA

LET GO

Koala medicine releases old grudges and difficult emotions and helps you offer forgiveness. What are you ready to be free of? What frustration, anger, or resentment can you finally give yourself permission to release today? This may be a feeling you hold against yourself or someone else. Releasing negative feelings frees up energetic space for new, more positive experiences and emotions. Just as the mother koala carries the young joey in its pouch until it's ready to be released, ask koala to help you let go of anything you no longer need to carry. Write down what you are ready to be free of and place the koala card by the list to help keep you focused and empowered in this intent.

INVOCATION TO ACTIVATE KOALA MEDICINE:

"Dear koala, if there is anything I've been carrying that is no longer serving my highest, greatest good, please lovingly show that to me. I am open to clearing old energies or emotions that hold me back. I am ready to open new space within me."

KOMODO DRAGON

ANSWER YOUR WAKE-UP CALL

Komodo dragon arrives to wake you up and shake things up! If you have been complacent, just going through the motions or sleepwalking through life, Komodo dragon will help you snap out of monotony. The brute strength of this fantastic lizard will break through unhealthy situations and blast you with new creative inspiration. Ask Komodo dragon to bless you with the power to take action! Place this card on your altar or bedside table and meditate on how you can be more present, engaged, and alive. Once you feel heart-centered and clear on what is best for you, ask Komodo dragon to be with you as you shake things up for the better.

INVOCATION TO ACTIVATE KOMODO DRAGON MEDICINE:

"Powerful Komodo dragon, thank you for waking me up. I ask that you keep me clear and resolute in what I need to do to open up a healthier life for myself. I receive your brute strength medicine now so I may be successful in this initiation."

LADYBUG

APPRECIATE BLESSINGS

Ladybug represents good fortune, and when it appears it means powerful blessings are making their way to you. Ladybug medicine is especially potent when you've been experiencing worry or are determined to see things through a negative lens. Are you aware of the infinite treasures and abundances all around you? What are you missing by only focusing on the things that aren't going exactly right? Take some time to reflect on how fleeting this Earth experience is and how incredible it is to be alive in this very moment. With ladybug by your side, let yourself fly to a higher consciousness so you can gain perspective on your circumstances and embrace the power of right now. Joy is your birthright.

INVOCATION TO ACTIVATE LADYBUG MEDICINE:

"Blessed ladybug, what a miracle this life is. Thank you for flying in to elevate my conscious awareness. Work with me to be present to the blessings that surround me."

LEECH

SHIFT FROM FEAR TO LOVE

Leech appears to remind you to keep your judgments in check. If you keep an open mind and heart, you might be pleasantly (or wildly) surprised. Leech represents the shift from fear to love. The leech is often misunderstood, but upon closer examination, we see it has complex biological systems and miraculous detoxification abilities that make it a truly remarkable being. Like all creatures, it has a sacred purpose, and that understanding can be transformed into reverence, respect, and love. With leech in mind, whose story can you get to know better? If someone's behavior has been confusing or off-putting, maybe it's time to have an openhearted conversation with them to try to better understand their inner world. Your ability to spiritually alchemize (shift from fear to love) can open your life to people and experiences beyond your wildest imagination.

INVOCATION TO ACTIVATE LEECH MEDICINE:

"Dear leech, thank you for teaching me to shift from fear to love. Work with me to allow my judgments to soften or completely dissolve. I allow my heart to be more open to unconditional love."

LEOPARD

EMBRACE YOUR UNIQUENESS

Leopard calls on you to unlock your unique personal medicine. Leopard reminds you to fully embody your true self, showing your unique spots with humility, honor, and grace. Are you hiding your soul's truth? What gifts, talents, and abilities have you been keeping from the world? Call upon leopard to assist you in building the confidence that lives within and releasing self-judgment so that you can share the medicine you are meant to share. Leopard also represents leadership, and leopard medicine can help you step into your power with heart, not ego.

INVOCATION TO ACTIVATE LEOPARD MEDICINE:

"Sacred leopard, I am ready to understand my divine power and lead from a place of humility, grace, and heart. I invite you to work with me so that I can share my truth with the world."

LION

EMBRACE HONESTY AND GENEROSITY

Lion represents honesty, generosity, and pure heart. Lion reminds you that you already have everything you need inside of you, and helps you unlock these attributes with grace so that you can share them with the world. If there is someone you should have an honest conversation with, ask lion to activate your courage, leadership, and integrity and go for it! If there's someone who could benefit from your generosity, then share your attention, energy, and resources with them without expectations or conditions. Call on lion's medicine to help you act from a place of love, knowing you will always be provided for.

INVOCATION TO ACTIVATE LION MEDICINE:

"Sacred lion, your leadership medicine is powerful, and I receive its energies into my heart now. Anywhere I can grow in honesty and generosity, keep my mind and heart keen and aware. Thank you."

LIZARD

WORK WITH DREAM TIME

Lizard represents adaptation and the magic of dream time. When lizard appears, it's time to pay close attention to your dreams, especially if you are currently going through any big changes. Call upon lizard to provide insight, medicine, or guidance while you sleep. Before you go to bed, set an intention for what you want to receive and ask lizard to work with you. If there is clarity you are seeking, deeper insight to compassionately understand an issue, solutions you want to gain in order to improve your relationship and more, ask lizard to provide answers. Keep a journal by your bed so that you can easily note any messages or visions that present in your dreams. If you are ready to initiate change or release something that you've clung to from your past, call on lizard to stay by your side as you adapt to a new way of living.

INVOCATION TO ACTIVATE LIZARD MEDICINE:

"Sacred lizard, please be with me during dream time. I invite in any messages, medicine, or guidance you wish to present to me to serve my greatest good and empower me during this time of great transformation. And so it is."

LLAMA

BE UNBOTHERED

Llama is deeply serene and present; it doesn't allow anyone to pull it out of its peace and power. Llama reminds you that you are already whole and beautiful. You just need to return yourself to these true places that already exist within you! You are absolutely worthy of living your grandest dreams, without concern for what others think. Llama brings you the medicines of joy, fun, being centered in your power, making time for laughter and play, and being mesmerized by the miracle that is your life. What step can you take today that will bring you back into authentic alignment with your soul and yourself? Llama will be with you.

INVOCATION TO ACTIVATE LLAMA MEDICINE:

"Sacred llama, help me remain in my peace and power, no matter what distractions come my way. I allow myself to be connected to the wholeness that lives within my now."

MACAW

CELEBRATE THE POWER OF EXPRESSION

Have you been holding back your energy for fear that it is "too much"? Have you been suppressing your voice in any way? The colorful and vocal macaw has flown into your field to help you examine the parts of yourself that are not being fully expressed. When you give yourself permission to speak your truth, to keep a song alive in your heart, then your life force grows stronger and you experience heightened moods and new creative energy. Take a moment now to reflect on whether your voice or the love in your heart feels fully open. If it doesn't, then what next step do you need to take to be in your truth?

INVOCATION TO ACTIVATE MACAW MEDICINE:

"Dear macaw, work with me to empower myself to fully express my abilities. Show me how I can find my voice and allow new inspiration to unfold in my life. I am grateful you showed up for me."

MANATEE

ALLOW FOR GENTLE TIMES

Manatees are incredibly large creatures, but they are gentle giants, gracefully swimming and serenely experiencing life. Manatee urges you to find a way, right now, to offer greater gentleness and loving compassion to your own being. There are times when you need to be proactive and energetic, and times when you need to rest, breathe deeply, and be extra gentle with yourself. To work with manatee, place your left hand on your heart and your right hand on your lower belly. Then, speak at least four gentle, kind, and loving statements about yourself. Savor this warm, tender energy. You can place the manatee card on your bathroom mirror to remind yourself to start every morning by repeating the loving statements or the invocation as you kindly meet your own gaze in the glass.

INVOCATION TO ACTIVATE MANATEE MEDICINE:

"Sacred manatee, empower me to move gently through my life and treat myself with compassion. If you have any heart-healing medicines you wish to provide to me, I invite them in fully at this time."

MONKEY

BRING IN MORE PLAYFULNESS

Monkey brings an air of playfulness, lightheartedness, and new energy into your life. Monkey also represents the ability to easily change directions, just as it does as it swings from tree to tree and branch to branch. Monkey shows up to remind you not to take life too seriously and urges you to step out of stale routines and comfort zones and embrace new adventures with curiosity and playfulness. If you have a lot of responsibilities, monkey reminds you that humor and flexibility will make your work more enjoyable.

INVOCATION TO ACTIVATE MONKEY MEDICINE:

"Dear monkey, I am grateful you have shown up to remind me that life can be filled with more ease, fun, and play. I invite you to guide me in receiving new inspiration around how to have a more adventurous life."

MOUNTAIN GOAT

KEEP GOING

Mountain goat is here to remind you to keep going, even when you are fatigued or considering giving up. Mountain goat represents remaining steadfast and persistent in reaching your goals and activating your greatest abilities! As you climb toward your goal with mountain goat by your side, remember to proceed at a sustainable pace that will not burn you out so that you can stay the course. Call upon mountain goat to give you the extra dose of ambition and determination you need to see your vision all the way through. You can do it!

INVOCATION TO ACTIVATE MOUNTAIN GOAT MEDICINE:

"Sacred mountain goat, I graciously receive your medicine to stay strong in reaching my goals. Help me feel invigorated on my quest. Empower me to stay the course with ambition and drive. And so it is."

MOUNTAIN LION

INITIATE EMBODIED LEADERSHIP

Mountain lion appears when you're in a position of leadership. A natural leader, mountain lion reminds you that the best way to lead is by truly walking the walk, leading from a place of pure integrity. That energy is born by constantly checking yourself and your motivations. Is there dysfunction, unhealthiness, or darkness present? It is imperative that you look closely at what's driving you. A true leader will do these uncomfortable integrity checks because leading from ego, force, or dysfunction can cause damage to those you lead. If you need to take a pause to reevaluate and reset, make the time.

Mountain lion reminds you that a true leader has integrity and honesty first and foremost with themselves.

INVOCATION TO ACTIVATE MOUNTAIN LION MEDICINE:

"Sacred mountain lion friend, thank you for this gut check. If I am leading with unhealthy energies, clearly let me know. If there is a way I can lead better, clearly let me know. Thank you."

MOUSE

RELEASE WORRY

Mouse appears to alleviate anxiety, overwhelm, and worry. When mouse shows up, it often means that you're stuck in a cycle of stress or experiencing nervous, scattered energy. When you're stuck in a stressful cycle, everything suffers—the quality of your health, the quality of your relationships, and the quality of your work—and it becomes difficult to access your true power. Work with mouse medicine to release stress and remember your innate power to calm yourself. Actively set aside time to do a short practice each day, such as meditating, chanting, journaling, spending time in nature, shamanic drumming, or praying. Place this card somewhere you can see it each morning to remind yourself of your commitment to doing something every day that brings you calm and allows you to hear the urgings and true power of your heart.

INVOCATION TO ACTIVATE MOUSE MEDICINE:

"Sacred mouse, if I am scurrying around with nervous energy, stress, or worry, remind me to make time for calm. I ask you to assist me in releasing worry so that I can operate from my true power. And so it is."

OCTOPUS

TRUST YOUR MULTITASKING POWERS

Have you been feeling overwhelmed, whether emotionally or with earthly tasks and to-do lists? Envision octopus's many arms, all tending to a different duty while in the water, and allow that vision to provide you with the confidence that you have incredible multitasking abilities as well. Bring yourself back to the present moment, close your eyes, and connect with your breath. Feel the ocean water clearing away any stress. Ask yourself what your priorities are and who you could ask to be one of your "arms" of support—who you could delegate a task to. Octopus shares with you its genius and ability to go with the flow. You have everything within you to make it through this fleeting chapter in your life.

INVOCATION TO ACTIVATE OCTOPUS MEDICINE:

"Sacred octopus friend, I appreciate and call upon your multitasking genius to help me remember that I am a powerful, capable being. With each breath I allow myself to be guided with ease to where I should focus. I trust in myself and your support. I can thrive in this."

OWL

ACTIVATE PSYCHIC INSIGHT

The owl represents seeing through the darkness to greater truths and deeper spiritual awareness. Owls can turn their heads 270 degrees, taking a wide view of their surroundings. This is symbolic of owl being a seer and having full awareness, even when things are shrouded in darkness. Ask yourself: "What truths am I avoiding because I fear the darkness?" One of the greatest things you can do for yourself is to illuminate the dark, shadowy parts of yourself and face them with bravery and open-mindedness. When you are honest with yourself, your life becomes one of truth and illumination rather than deceit and confusion.

INVOCATION TO ACTIVATE OWL MEDICINE:

"Sacred owl, I allow your potent insight to work with me. I am ready to clear darkness, fog, and confusion to allow for clarity and illumination."

PEACOCK

SHARE YOUR TRUE COLORS

Peacock represents creative expression, self-love, and authenticity. Peacock shows up to help you express and embrace your true, authentic self. Close your eyes and picture a majestic peacock spreading its brightly colored tail feathers, letting them fan open far and wide for all to see. Let your eyes rest on the awe-inspiring display of natural beauty. This is the energetic essence that peacock wishes to share with you now. If you've been hiding your true colors and creative gifts from yourself or the world, now is the time to express them. Peacock and its fierce self-love medicine are with you. Do not fear that being your most magnificent self has to equate to ego or bragging. You have the ability to shine with humility, grace, and honor.

INVOCATION TO ACTIVATE PEACOCK MEDICINE:

"Dear peacock, thank you for being a true representation of how to express your beauty and truth. I am now ready to do the same. I allow your medicine in to empower me to share my authentic colors with the world. I now trust this process."

PENGUIN

ACHIEVE HARMONY

Penguin represents balance, stability, and alignment. If you've been feeling off-kilter recently, take a moment to check in with yourself regarding how much balance and harmony are present in your life. Have you been pushing yourself too hard and not taking proper time to nourish and care for yourself? Have you been giving away more than you're getting back in return? Identify the places where things have fallen out of alignment. If you've let the pendulum swing too far in one direction, this is the time to recalibrate. Close your eyes and imagine a penguin surefootedly making its way across ice. What first step can you take today that will begin to restore some balance to your life? Be respectful and kind with yourself during this process.

INVOCATION TO ACTIVATE PENGUIN MEDICINE:

"Dear penguin friend, thank you for being my wake-up call that I need better balance and alignment in my life. I invite you to work with me in restoring balance and harmony within myself and in my heart. Empower my first steps in this process today."

PORCUPINE

TRUST OPENHEARTED VULNERABILITY

Porcupine has the incredible ability to face things with openheartedness and vulnerability or turn its back and lift its quills (defenses) up. While it may feel safer to move through life with your defenses up, when you close your heart, you close yourself off from authentic, loving, expansive experiences. When was the last time you faced something head-on and vulnerably shared your feelings or truths with someone else? Remember, even if you are taking part in sensitive or challenging conversations, you can lead with gentleness and heart rather than fear and mistrust. Pay close attention to any tendencies you have to get "prickly" with your own quills or defensive—and notice what's triggering those reactions. Can you recommit to opening up to people you trust at a gentle pace that feels right for you?

INVOCATION TO ACTIVATE PORCUPINE MEDICINE:

"Sacred porcupine, thank you for reminding me that being tough and defensive can close me off to deep conversations and experiences. Thank you for reminding me of the potency of openly, honestly sharing and being vulnerable. Work with me so that I can share my truths and open myself to miracles."

PRAYING MANTIS

ENGAGE IN PRAYER AND SURRENDER

Praying mantis represents divine timing, prayer, and surrender. Praying mantis shows up when it's time to take your spiritual or mindfulness practices deeper, especially if you have been feeling impatient with something in your life. Perhaps you wish you had an answer for something right now or you wish a goal or intention you've set had already come to fruition. The easiest way to encourage patience, especially when you're eager for something to happen or physically manifest, is to surrender the goal in prayer. Holding this card, say a prayer for the dream you want to manifest. Ask that the prayer be answered in a way that will serve the greatest good, and know that you will be given insight and instructions on when to take your next step. It is all about trusting divine timing.

INVOCATION TO ACTIVATE PRAYING MANTIS MEDICINE:

"Dear praying mantis, I am ready to surrender to the rhythms and instructions of the Universe and my soul. I ask that you reveal to me how to be in a strong and trusting cocreative relationship with Source. Empower my prayers and reveal any clarity that will illuminate my pathway forward."

RABBIT

ACTIVATE FERTILITY

Rabbit shows up when you're ready to bring something new into the world. Rabbit represents fertility and birthing of a new life force. Rabbit medicine can surely pertain to the birthing of a soul in human form, but it can also be harnessed to birth a new project, opportunity, or insight. Oftentimes, when something new is on the horizon, it can kick up fear. It is important that you act quickly to avoid letting fear hold you back or paralyze you from making moves. Call on rabbit to activate your ability to make quick decisions. Let rabbit medicine help you birth something beautiful.

INVOCATION TO ACTIVATE RABBIT MEDICINE:

"Sacred rabbit, if fears have been holding me back or clouding my vision, reveal to me how to transcend them. I commit to moving into action and taking steps to birth something new to the world immediately. Empower me in these freeing processes."

RACCOON

REMOVE THE MASK

Raccoon, with its mask-like markings and dexterous hands, represents personal change and being of service. When raccoon appears, consider the unique potential for good that you carry and what heart-centered shifts you can make in your life to help heal this planet. Raccoon reminds you to explore and embrace your personal gifts—remember, you do not have to be what you've been before; you have permission to shift and evolve in whatever ways suit your soul. If you've been wearing a mask to hide your soul's calling, now is the time to show your true identity. The world will be better for it.

INVOCATION TO ACTIVATE RACCOON MEDICINE:

"Dear raccoon, work with me to remove any masks that are concealing the true me. I am ready to share my truth with the world and focus on being of service to others in order to leave behind a positive legacy. And so it is."

RHINOCEROS

GET OUT OF YOUR OWN WAY

Have you lost sight of the incredible abundance and miracles in your life? The rhinoceros helps you blast through mental barriers so that you can confidently move forward with strength and energy. Consider whether you're allowing negative thinking, a defeatist or victim mentality, or low self-worth to get in your way or drain your energy. Be real with yourself! It's now time for you to confidently celebrate all the glorious things you have to be grateful for. Stop letting fear hold you back. You are not a victim! You are an empowered, fierce being blessed with many gifts. It is time to charge ahead with rhino by your side.

INVOCATION TO ACTIVATE RHINOCEROS MEDICINE:

"Powerful rhino, infuse me with confidence so that I may see the abundance in my life. Allow me to be enlightened and strengthened by what I've previously endured. Work with me to see the bounty of miracles that surround me so that I may invite even more in and get out of my own way. And so it is."

ROADRUNNER

TRANSFORM YOUR ENERGY

Roadrunner has a keen ability to make fast decisions, shift into action, and take off, and roadrunner medicine can work quickly to transform your energy. If you have been in a rut, procrastinating, or letting yourself wallow in an unfavorable emotion for an extended amount of time, roadrunner is your guide to getting unstuck. To work with roadrunner medicine, close your eyes and take off into the cosmos, letting your mind explore the infinite space surrounding you. Journey farther and farther out into the void, simply exploring the open, forever space. While you're exploring the cosmos, consider what new emotion you'd like to experience in order to feel less stuck. Now imagine locating that emotion on your exploration, and see how it transforms your energy. Once those feelings land in your body, open your eyes.

INVOCATION TO ACTIVATE ROADRUNNER MEDICINE:

"Sacred roadrunner friend, when I am stuck in a cycle of suffering or low energy, remind me of my infinite nature and my ability to quickly take off. Empower me to find my way out of ruts so that I can confidently and swiftly move toward my dreams."

ROOSTER

REMEMBER LAUGHTER AND JOY

Roosters may have a fierce side, but their medicine also brings laughter, joy, and healthy relationships to your life. Have you ever heard a loud and proud rooster's crow that sounds just like laughing? It's an incredibly medicinal sound and it reminds you that you should never dim your joy or exuberance for life for anyone. Surround yourself with friends who honor your unique energy. Healthy people will celebrate your happiness (they may even want to know what your secret is!). If you're afraid of someone leaving or not liking you because you are joyful and thriving, consider whether that person is someone worth your precious time and energy. Rooster reminds you of the vital importance of having relationships where you are embraced for being yourself, without holding anything back. You should not have to hide your truth for anyone.

INVOCATION TO ACTIVATE ROOSTER MEDICINE:

"Dear rooster, thank you for reminding me to be an open conduit for the joy and exuberance that wants to move through me. I commit to remembering that the joyful light and expression that is me, is a gift to the world and to never dim it for anyone."

SEAGULL

TIDY UP

Just as you may recall a time when you've witnessed a seagull going for food or trash at the beach, seagull appears when it's time to tidy up. This could pertain to a variety of literal and figurative areas of your life—your home, your relationships, your mental clutter, your emotional attachments. Work with seagull medicine to identify the things that are taking up space in your mind and life without providing benefit. Find a quiet place to sit and gaze at this card for a few moments, then ask yourself, "What needs cleaning up in my life?" Listen to whatever arises, and consider how you can commit to cleaning up. Then make a plan to act. It's not easy to clear the debris you've been holding on to, but it's worth it. When you clear out the objects, emotions, and relationships that no longer serve you, you show yourself self-respect and make space for new energy and new experiences.

INVOCATION TO ACTIVATE SEAGULL MEDICINE:

"Sacred seagull friend, I invite you to work with me to keep my energy and life clear of debris. I know this will give me a renewed sense of self-respect and energy. I am ready."

SEAL

FIND HEART CONNECTION

Seal appears to help you strengthen your connection to your heart so that you can make heart-centered decisions. When you're truly connected to your heart, its intelligence and wisdom will guide you toward your true power and soul calling. As seals are incredibly talented vocalists, singing is a beautiful way to activate and honor seal medicine. Find a quiet, private spot and place this card in front of you. Sing whatever feels good—you can make up a song, hum, chant, or put on music and sing along to a favorite artist. The power of song will open revitalized, dynamic energies within you and forge stronger connections between your head and heart.

INVOCATION TO ACTIVATE SEAL MEDICINE:

"Sacred seal, I am ready to listen to my heart. I trust that cultivating a heart connection will allow me to be most connected to my power, the Divine, and truth. I allow the sweet song of your medicine to enter into me and open the pathways between my heart and Source."

SHARK

FLOW FORWARD

Shark appears to help you find pure flow with the Universe. Shark's graceful, confident swim reminds you to stay open and adaptable, rather than resisting what life throws your way. When the waters of life are choppy or the current is moving against you, work with shark medicine to inquire what lessons you can learn and how this experience can help you further expand into your power so that you can respond to any situation with grace. Shark medicine allows you to become at one with all that is, flowing forward in a state of continual learning, openness, and love.

INVOCATION TO ACTIVATE SHARK MEDICINE:

"Honorable shark friend, I invite you to continue teaching me to swim in alignment with the Universe. If I find myself resisting what is presenting, may you bring me back to awareness so that I can stay open and inquisitive. And so it is."

SHEEP

LEAD COMMUNITY UNITY

Sheep asks you to open your pure, golden heart energy to uplift your community, especially when you've been too focused on yourself. When sheep appears, consider how you can connect with others through gatherings, acts of service, and thoughtful outreach. This could be hosting a monthly moon circle, working in the community garden, or starting a volunteer cleanup crew in your neighborhood. Sheep invites you to step into a leadership role within your community so that the people around you feel loved, held, and nourished. Similar to sheep and their ability to bond and move as one in their flock to protect members from predators, when you work to build a healthy community, it will hold you in return.

INVOCATION TO ACTIVATE SHEEP MEDICINE:

"Sacred sheep, when I become too self-serving, remind me it's time to reconnect with my community. I am ready to see how I can serve the greater whole, for the greater good. I invite you into my pure heart to show me the way."

SKUNK

SET HEALTHY BOUNDARIES

Just as skunk can remain jovial and only spray when a true threat is detected, skunk appears when it's time to put healthy boundaries into place. When people disrespect your time, energy, or emotional well-being, call on skunk to help you stand up for yourself and set necessary boundaries to protect your energy. If someone repeatedly dishonors you, demands too much from you, or crosses a line after you've asked them not to, it's time to be clear they no longer have the same access to your precious energy. If you feel that communicating a new boundary is the healthiest course of action, don't avoid that conversation simply because it may be uncomfortable—the long-term benefits and self-respect you'll feel will outweigh the momentary discomfort. Skunk can also be your ally if you put up too many barriers in your life. If you tend to be overly defensive in an attempt to protect your heart, work with skunk to reveal whether you're really protecting yourself or preventing yourself from having deep, vulnerable experiences and relationships.

INVOCATION TO ACTIVATE SKUNK MEDICINE:

"Dear skunk friend, work with me to set healthy boundaries so that I am surrounded by people who respect my energy and positively enhance my life and intimate relationships."

SLOTH

SEEK NATURE'S WISDOM

Sloth represents a connection to nature and a thoughtful, intentional approach to life. When you feel overwhelmed or scattered, sloth medicine helps you tune in to the wisdom of the natural world for relief and perspective. Being in nature, observing its rhythms and pace, is a natural balm. Sloths make their homes in trees, and that's where they receive their nourishment and rest. To connect with sloth, place the sloth card in your pocket or bag and find a place where you can see a tree—whether it's your backyard or a local park. Sit quietly, observing all the details of the tree—its colors, its leaves and branches, the sound it makes in the wind. Like the sloth, you too can receive rest and nourishment from the tree.

INVOCATION TO ACTIVATE SLOTH MEDICINE:

"Sacred sloth ally, thank you for this reminder to nourish myself in nature and return to the present moment. I allow the whispers of the wind, the power of the land, and the wisdom of the trees to be my teachers today. And so it is."

SNAIL

LEAN INTO TRUE INTIMACY

Snail appears to help you experience true intimacy. Sometimes that may mean slowing things down a bit while you're dating or in a relationship. Consider whether you're truly in tune with your needs and desires, or whether you're just going through the motions. Intimacy is nuanced and personal; it requires deep communication and connection. Allow the wisdom within your heart to guide you, and move from there with deliberate intention—do not rush things. Take as many pauses as you need to check in and make sure that you are being honored on a soul level and treating others with the respect and care they deserve. Enjoy the process of something slowly unfolding.

INVOCATION TO ACTIVATE SNAIL MEDICINE:

"Dear snail, anytime I am getting ahead of the ideal pace of divine timing, remind me to breathe, be present, and slow down. Work with me to ensure I am taking the time to tune in to my own needs so that I can be in relationships that honor me."

SNAKE

WELCOME HIGHER GUIDANCE

When snake appears, it's a sign that change is on the horizon and that new spiritual, sexual, or creative forces are rising within you. Snake signifies a time of transformation: Your old snakeskin is ready to be shed so that you can move forward with newfound power and clarity. When snake beckons, it is important for you to be more in tune than ever with your higher self. Connect with your higher self through practices like meditation or breathwork, and listen to the intuitive messages that present. What gifts and powers are hiding beneath your old skin, ready to reveal themselves to the world?

INVOCATION TO ACTIVATE SNAKE MEDICINE:

"Sacred snake, I hear your call for me to begin a process of transformation. I open myself to the new life force that wants to birth within me. May this all be done to serve the greatest good, with healthy integration and embodiment and ease."

SPIDER

CREATE MAGIC

Spider appears to help you weave magic. Consider the intricacy and beauty of a spiderweb, a shimmery world in its own right. What magical world awaits you? Spider appears to share that a new possibility for your life awaits. Take a moment now to close your eyes and see or feel how a unique new web of magic is opening up for you at this time. What opportunity can you step into? What idea that you've had feels ready to be expressed to the world? Even if the magical possibilities presenting seem unfathomable, "too good to be true," or surprising in some way, trust that you can allow the new medicine opening up for you to be tasted and experienced one step, one thread, at a time. Go for it!

INVOCATION TO ACTIVATE SPIDER MEDICINE:

"Sacred spider, work with me to trust in the new magic opening up in my life. Infuse your special medicine into the new worlds emerging, so that I may welcome what is to come with honor, sacredness, and integrity. And so it is."

STARFISH

FIND INTERNAL VALIDATION

Starfish enters when you need to stay strong in your authenticity and truth, despite what others may say or think. This is especially important if you have people-pleasing tendencies. Sometimes, our fear of other people's judgments, expectations, and disappointments can be paralyzing, but if you remember the starfish's ability to regenerate a limb if bitten off, you can also remember your ability to regenerate your authenticity and truth when someone attempts to cut off your power or light. When you feel yourself contorting to align with someone else's sense of you, call on starfish medicine to help you stay strong in internal validation.

Starfish reminds you to trust in your unique sacred path, knowing that at the end of the day, being right within yourself and in alignment with Great Spirit/Source is far more valuable than someone else's acceptance. Starfish also reminds you to show others the same respect and non-judgment in return.

INVOCATION TO ACTIVATE STARFISH MEDICINE:

"Sacred starfish friend, help keep me strong when fear of judgment or criticism arises. Support my ability to feel peace and joy as I walk my own unique path. And so it is."

STINGRAY

DISCOVER PEACE AND CALM

Stingray bestows calm when you most need it. When you find yourself in a situation that triggers feelings of anger, frustration, or stress, stingray medicine helps you take a pause and connect to calm before responding. Often, when a sudden rush of emotions rises within you, the immediate response is to let those feelings burst out as a gut reaction. However, if you can think of stingray's ability to move peacefully with the sway of the tide, oftentimes resting, buried in the sand, and sit with that burst you're feeling for just a moment and let the kicked up sand within you settle, you can avoid unnecessary drama and conflict. Call on stingray to help you connect to calm by closing your eyes and breathing deeply and imagining a stingray slowly moving along the ocean floor. This short visualization can quickly soothe you, allowing you to respond with intention rather than react from a place of heightened emotion.

INVOCATION TO ACTIVATE STINGRAY MEDICINE:

"Sacred stingray, thank you for reminding me of the importance of choosing peace and calm over drama and pain. Work with me to help me find my center during times of angst or despair. Allow me to respond in healthy ways rather than reacting hastily."

STORK

RECEIVE BLESSINGS AND GIFTS

Stork enters your life to bestow beautiful gifts of abundance, good fortune, and prosperity. You might become so distracted by the stresses of daily life that you fail to see opportunities for nourishment and support. Consider what blessings are presenting, especially around your home and/or family life. Perhaps you're finally ready to get that new puppy, maybe you're making healthy strides in forgiving or healing a family rift, or perhaps you've decided to invite family and friends over to the home you've spent months renovating—allow the iconic medicine of stork to enter fully and deliver and birth more good fortune for you!

INVOCATION TO ACTIVATE STORK MEDICINE:

"Dear stork, I am open to receiving the good fortune and love you want to bestow in my life. I invite your healing medicine pertaining to roots and home to be delivered, and I am truly grateful to you for blessing me with these gifts."

SWAN

AWAKEN ARTISTIC SPIRIT

Swan represents art and poetry. Swan swims gracefully forward to signal that it is time for you to tap into your artistic spirit. To work with swan medicine, spend at least 10 minutes today devoted to opening up your creativity. Write a poem, tell a story, paint a picture, sing a song. There are so many ways to be creative, so explore what it means to you without self-judgment. When you allow creative energy to be unleashed, you reconnect to who you are at your core. Don't be afraid to share your artistic or poetic expressions with trusted friends—share your light with people you love and they will be inspired too. Ask swan to support you in this endeavor.

INVOCATION TO ACTIVATE SWAN MEDICINE:

"Dearest swan, thank you for being with me as I share beauty and art with the world. Today I will make time to create by _____, and I ask that you be with me to empower this process. If my gifts are meant to shine in a group, allow this to happen with grace, ease, and confidence."

TIGER

EMBRACE TOUCH AND SENSUALITY

In shamanic medicine, tiger represents sensuality and the power of touch. Does your body need touch? Check in with yourself to see how long it's been since you've connected with another person through touch—whether it's a hug from a friend, a relaxing massage, or a loving experience with a partner. Human touch is revitalizing and sustaining; it can move old energy or emotions when you're feeling stressed, overwhelmed, or disconnected. The element of water works strongly with both tiger and sensuality, as tigers are powerful swimmers, so you can also activate tiger medicine through time in the water, even if you're simply soaking in a bath. As you connect with tiger, allow your soul to show you what new healing, sensual adventures it wishes to go on. Journal about what is revealed.

INVOCATION TO ACTIVATE TIGER MEDICINE:

"Tiger ally, work with me in opening up new gateways of connection and passion in my life. I allow your sensual teachings to be sent my way, and I am excited to see what new experiences will reveal. Thank you for generously sharing your power."

TURTLE

EVOKE ANCIENT GROUNDED POWER

Turtles are ancient beings and they carry the ancient wisdom and powers of Mother Earth. They are believed to have existed 200 million years ago, and some species can live to be several hundred years old. Turtle reveals to remind you that you too carry ancient wisdoms, medicines, and knowledge within you. You are wiser than you give yourself credit for at times. Turtle reminds you that you are exactly where you need to be, grounding you in deep wisdom that is ready to emerge from you at this time. To connect with turtle's grounding medicine, lay on your back, ideally directly on the earth or a wood floor, and take deep, fulfilling breaths. With each exhalation, imagine any stresses or concerns being released down into Mother Earth. Thank her for receiving and transmuting these energies into love.

INVOCATION TO ACTIVATE TURTLE MEDICINE:

"Sacred turtle, thank you for representing the ancient wisdoms and medicines of this beautiful planet. Work with me to help me feel more grounded so that I can safely let my power and knowledge be shared. I trust in this present moment."

WHALE

COMMUNICATE CLEARLY

Whales, known for their beautiful, otherworldly singing, can enhance your ability to express and communicate. When whale shows up for you, consider whom you could have better communication with. Is there someone your intuition has been telling you to check in with or give more attention to? This is your wake-up call to listen and act on those nudges. Because whale also represents healing ancestral or lineage traumas, you can call on whale to help you have healing conversations with family members. Be honest with yourself and open the communication portal. You have the most powerful ally by your side now.

INVOCATION TO ACTIVATE WHALE MEDICINE:

"Sacred whale, clear any anxiety or procrastination around communicating with others. Thank you for sharing your powerful ancient wisdom of song with me so that I can connect with others with integrity, honesty, and love. I receive your medicine with honor."

WOLF

STEP INTO SOVEREIGNTY

Wolf represents independence and sovereignty: the ability to be healthily whole and complete within oneself, not needing to look outside of oneself for anything, including fulfillment. Because wolf is secure and confident in itself, it is also comfortable with its place within the pack, honoring and respecting the elders who lead the way and set the pace. Wolf reminds you that putting in the work to attain sovereign union with your own self is the key that unlocks infinite and miraculous treasures in all ways for the rest of your life. When you have nothing to prove, you can joyously be at one with the community. The powers of the moon (especially the full moon) and ritual are also greatly tied into wolf medicine, so speak the invocation or do any other honoring practice, such as a releasing or letting go ceremony on the next full moon.

INVOCATION TO ACTIVATE WOLF MEDICINE:

"Sacred wolf teacher, I am ready to anchor myself in total confidence of who I am and do so with divine humility. Please show me the rituals and practices that will bring me into embodiment of my sovereignty. And so it is."

ZEBRA

BREAK FREE OF THE BOX

The wild and wonderful zebra comes galloping in to remind you to not let anyone (yourself included) put you into a box. Zebra's unique stripes represent individuality and remind you that you are a multifaceted, multidimensional, wondrous creature who can evolve infinitely. Never let anyone else define you or tell you who you can and cannot be. When someone else expands or grows, celebrate them and their journey! When you expand and grow, celebrate yourself! Stand confidently and boldly in your uniqueness and do not let unfair or unhealthy criticisms take up space in your being.

INVOCATION TO ACTIVATE ZEBRA MEDICINE:

"Dear zebra, thank you for showing your stripes so beautifully and inspiring me to boldly claim my unique and special path and existence. Work with me to help me go deeper into the layers within myself and celebrate expansion. When I know me, I know the world."

GLOSSARY:

Earth mission: The way in which your soul experiences spiritual evolution during your incarnation on Earth. Your Earth mission is what you are called to teach and be a conduit for during your time on Earth.

Great Spirit: The pure and unconditionally loving creator of all that is.

Source: Also known as Source Consciousness, this is the source of divine guidance, presenting us with information in infinite shapes and forms.

Spiritual alchemy: Spiritual alchemy is the ability to healthily work with a challenging or difficult experience and pivot from a place of fear or pain to a place of greater love and embodiment. In short, spiritual alchemy is the process of turning a painful experience into an opportunity for ascension.

Transmutation: Transmutation occurs when experiences of hardship become growth lessons for your soul. When something is transmuted, a challenging situation becomes a teaching that allows for a positive evolution in your life experience. For example, "She was able to transmute the pain of her breakup and emerge from the experience with greater self-honor and a healthier lifestyle."